To the Welte's,

Thanks for all and encouragments and our time together at Christ Lutheran!

I miss you and hope that your life in Northern California is one of meaning and good ministry!

Larry

David R. Ellingson and Darcy D. Jensen convincingly show the intimate connections between "a life in the spirit" and "a life in the body." In a very concrete and practical way they illustrate the importance of wholistic living, a living in which deep prayer, healthy eating habits, and balanced physical exercises are all important elements in the maturation process of the person. An excellent book for all those who do not want to separate holiness from wholeness.

Henri J. M. Nouwen

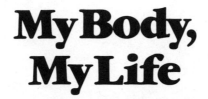

My Body, My Life

My Body, My Life

How you can combine
prayer, praise, and the
spiritual with work,
play, and the physical
for a healthier and more
joyful Christian life.

David R. Ellingson
& Darcy D. Jensen

AUGSBURG Publishing House • Minneapolis

MY BODY, MY LIFE

Scripture quotations unless otherwise noted are from the Revised Standard Version of the Bible, copyright 1946, 1952, and 1971 by the Division of Christian Education of the National Council of Churches.

Photos: Strix Pix, 26, 101; Hedgecoth Photographers, 32; Tom Mcguire, 36; RNS, 41, 47, 96; D. Michael Hostetler, 53; Bob Combs, 58; Paul Buddle, 65; Paul Schrock, 72; Vivienne, 76; Rohn Engh, 83; Jean-Claude Lejeune, 89; Bruce Jennings, 119.

MANUFACTURED IN THE UNITED STATES OF AMERICA

Contents

Experience Guide

As a way of helping you make well-planned progress in your physical and spiritual growth, we invite you to complete the following "Personal Inventory" before you read this book. It is intended to help you identify areas of strength and needed growth. Then, as you read further, you may take active steps toward wholeness in specific areas of your life. The "Nutritional Charts" and "Self-Directed Exercise Program" are to help you begin the principles in this book right away.

Take time after reading each chapter to try the "Experiences and Exercises" at the end. They are concrete ways to guide your journey. After you have finished reading this book, return to the "Personal

Inventory." Use it to reexamine where you now are along the path toward wholeness. Then use the "Month's Measure" chart to plan your continuing efforts and goals. Finally, promise yourself that you will review your progress within six months or a year to see how it's going.

Personal inventory

general information

flexibility_____(This is measured in + or – inches. Sit on the floor with legs outstretched and knees flat to the floor. Try to touch your toes. Yours will be a minus measurement if you cannot reach your toes. Yours will be a positive measurement if you stretch beyond.)

age_____

% body fat (if known)_____

pulse_____

blood pressure_____

weight_____

body frame (circle one): large   medium   small

waist_____

current level of health_____

special health problems_____

_____

When was the last time you felt the fittest or healthiest that you had ever felt?

_____

_____

Describe yourself at that time_____

_____

_____

_____

yourself

What is your earliest memory about your own body?

_____

_____

What were you told about your body as you grew up?_____

_____

What is your first memory about your spirit?

_____

_____

the Bible and prayer

Describe the Scripture passages on the body which first come to mind._____

_____

_____

What is your understanding of the Bible's general opinion of the body?_____

_____

_____

How has that view influenced you?_____

_____

_____

Define *prayer:*_____

_____

Define *meditation:*_____

_____

Describe your style of prayer:_____

_____

_____

How often do you pray?_____
Where do you pray?_____
When do you pray?_____
If you meditate, describe your style of meditation:

_____

_____

_____

food
Describe your "average" meal:_____

_____

_____

Describe your dietary habits:_____

_____

_____

When do you eat?_____
How often do you eat?_____
How much do you eat?_____
Why do you eat?_____

Do you ever eat or drink to ease personal tension or anxiety?_____

Describe your drinking and smoking habits:

_____

_____

How often do you smoke or drink?_____

When do you smoke or drink?_____

How much do you smoke or drink?_____

Why do you smoke or drink?_____

_____

_____

movement

Give a brief history of exercise in your life:

_____

_____

_____

_____

_____

What do you like *least* about physical exercise?

_____

_____

What do you like *most* about physical exercise?

_____

_____

Which physical activity do you enjoy participating in the most?_____

What is your current level of activity?_____

_____

How do you exercise?_____

_____

_____

_____

How often (per week) do you exercise?_____

Why do you exercise?_____

_____

_____

_____

What does the word *discipline* mean to you?

_____

_____

play

What do you do to re-create?_____

_____

_____

_____

How do you most often spend your leisure time?

_____

_____

_____

How do you now play?_____

_____

_____

In what ways might the Christian faith be re-creative

or playful?_____

_____

_____

How might your play better express your Christian identity?_____

_____

_____

Nutritional charts
- *The basic four.*

---

milk, cheese, ice cream, yogurt
    children up to 11 years   2½ cups per day
    adolescents   4 cups
    adults   1½ cups
    pregnant and
       nursing mothers   3 to 4 cups

---

meat, poultry, seafood, eggs, legumes, nuts, peanut
    butter, two 2/3 oz. servings

---

vegetables, fruits
    four servings, including
    one high in vitamin C and
    one high in vitamin A

---

cereals, breads
    four servings

The basic four food groups approach is useful as a general guide, but we should be aware that in the way it is often used, it tends to affirm our overconsumption of protein.

● *Building a simpler diet.*[1]

What should we eat and what should we not eat to free resources for hungry people and to improve our own health? General guidelines which take into account world food and energy needs, good nutrition, and food costs can be summarized this way:

eat more

whole grains	*legumes (dried beans)*
rice	soybeans
wheat	dried peas
barley	lentils
rye	peanuts
oats	
corn	
millet	

nuts & seeds	*vegetables and fruits*
(inexpensive,	(inexpensive locally

---

[1] Reprinted by permission from *More-With-Less Cookbook* by Doris Janzen Longacre, copyright 1976 by Herald Press, Scottdale, Pa. 15683.

locally grown   grown varieties or
varieties)   homegrown and preserved)

use carefully
  eggs, milk, cheeses, yogurt, seafoods, poultry,
    meats

avoid
  superprocessed and convenience foods
  superpackaged foods
  foods heavy in refined sugar
    and saturated fats
  foods shipped long distances,
    especially under refrigeration

• A *vegetarian diet*
  (this diet is "lacto-ovo vegetarian" because it
    includes dairy products)

Basic to a sound vegetarian diet is combining the
right amounts of various foods to get complete protein. The following formulas and chart should help
in understanding this type of diet.

To achieve complete protein one must combine:
1. *grains* (cereals, pasta, rice, corn, etc.)
   plus *legumes* (beans, peas, lentils)
2. *grains* plus *milk products*
3. *seeds* (sesame or sunflower)
   plus *legumes* (beans, peas, or lentils)

How much of each is needed?[2]

1 part legumes	and	2 parts milk
2 parts legumes	and	3 parts seeds
1 part legumes	and	3 parts whole grains
4 parts milk	and	3 parts whole grains
1 part milk (scant)	and	1 part seeds
1 part milk (scant)	and	1 part peanuts
1 part milk	and	1 part potato

Self-directed exercise program

Pick the kind of activity that you enjoy. Perhaps a combination will create more pleasure, through variety. Often a partner will be both a reminder and a companion in exercise. Set some reasonable goals (*less* is better to start with) and find a time which you *will* set aside for exercise. Remember, you give many hours to mental activity. An hour a day for physical exercise is not much to ask. Plan warm-up time (stretching) and cool-down time, along with the exercise itself. You'll be surprised how quickly this activity will become a good habit.

The following table from "How Much Exercise

---

[2] From *Cooking With Conscience* by Alice Benjamin and Harriet Corrigan. Copyright © 1975 by Vineyard Books, Inc. Used by permission of The Seabury Press, Inc.

Is Enough?" by Michael L. Pollock offers some helpful guidelines for your planning:[3]

*Recommendations for exercise prescription for
healthy adults*

frequency	3 to 5 days a week
intensity	60% to 90% of maximum heart rate (subtract your age from 220; multiply by .6, .7, or .8; count pulse for 15 seconds right after exercise; multiply by 4; multiply this by .93 plus 16.32 to get the rate at which you should exercise for 15-60 minutes)
duration	15 to 60 minutes (continuous)
activity	running, jogging, walking, bicycling, swimming, or endurance sport activities
initial level of fitness	high = higher work load low = lower work load

NOTE: *Before beginning any new exercise program
it is always wise to consult with a physician.*

---

[3] Reprinted from *The Physician and Sports Medicine*, a Mc-
Graw-Hill publication.

A month's measure

It has been said that the three keys to a long and happy life are a positive attitude, sound nutrition, and good exercise. This chart seeks to help you to see the correlation between these three principles. After completing the "Personal Inventory" you can begin the exercises and experiences at the end of each chapter. Use the graph on the next page to help you see the interrelationships and progress you experience. It might be helpful to use a different colored line for each area (attitude—blue; nutrition—red; exercise—green).

Week 1	Week 2	Week 3	Week 4

Level of activity/progress

1

The Body
and Spirituality

The story is a universal one. From our earliest
years we struggle to understand our bodies. What are
they? How do we use them? Why do they cause us
pain? More often than not, our bodies have gotten
us into trouble. Almost everyone has at least one
childhood memory of being spanked for being too
active in church or being teased for being too tall,
too short, too fat, too skinny, or having a face full
of acne. Most of us were convinced long ago that
our bodies were too undisciplined, awkward, and
ugly.

Each of us has learned to control, change, or deny
our bodies. None of us has fared very well at this.
Young girls were to give up the scuffed knees of the

"tomboy" years and become feminine. In becoming more "ladylike" they learned to be physically inactive, studious, timid, and always pretty. Young boys, on the other hand, were expected to live lives of dirty jeans, tattered tennis shoes, and baseball gloves. Tall boys were to be good basketball players. Large boys were destined for football. The rest were unfortunately left out.

By the time all of us had reached our teenage years, our minds were filled with unhealthy images about our bodies. And the rules of behavior established to control our bodies cemented those impressions. We had labels aplenty to describe the ways in which people conformed to those body rules. Those who couldn't completely deny their bodies were jocks, peanut brains, muscle heads, and dumbbells. Those who developed in scholarly ways were known as eggheads, wimps, bookworms, and teachers' pets. A third group were those who took church especially seriously. They were goody-goodys, space pilots, fundies, holy rollers, and Bible-thumpers. No one lived very comfortably with such labels. And the body-image problem continued to grow for everyone.

When we reached adulthood we thought we would finally be able to set some of our own body rules. Yet our heritage of earlier years lingered on. We discovered that we could never really free ourselves from the prejudices toward our bodies that we learned in our youth. Our lives continued to be infected with a tragically negative view of our bodies, and therefore of ourselves.

The cult of the body

In response to this heritage of bad feelings we have developed numerous life-styles to overcompensate. For example, one's body may not be that good, but a little adjustment here and a little alteration there may make it presentable. By changing our exterior appearance we can at least camouflage our bad body images. From cradle to grave we try to alter our appearance with cosmetics, illusionary fashions, and concealment. By using this cover-up or that highlighter we can pretend that our bodies are attractive and appealing.

Our society worships "perfect" young bodies. Beauty contests, television shows, and advertisements prey upon our attraction to the beautiful. We who do not fit such an image become further alienated from our bodies, and in the process the human body is cheapened beyond all our fears of ugliness. No longer knowing what a healthy body image really is, we vacillate between hate and love. Worst of all, we make everyone (including ourselves) into objects for scorn and personal gratification. We have become victims of the cult of the body.

The cult of the spirit

Others, usually religious people, are vulnerable to a different error—the cult of the spirit. For them the body has become a thorn in their spiritual flesh. It's a prison for the spirit. Trapped inside this cumbersome hulk, the spirit is constantly at war with the body's desires.

Those of an earlier age intentionally abused their bodies. Today we ignore and deny them. We ignore our bodies in obesity and sedentary living. We deny them by overwork and stressful living. We see our physical life as punishment or testing of our spirits. And what our spirits really want is release.

Both of these cults—the cult of the body and the cult of the spirit—are gravely in error. Either way, the body *and* the spirit are both imprisoned.

The roots of our problem

There are two root causes of our distorted, negative image of our bodies. First, we have tended to believe that the Bible separates the body and the spirit, setting them in opposition to each other. Such a reading of the Bible prevents us from seeing the unity of life. We are hard-pressed to speak meaningfully of human persons as wholesome, positive unities of body and spirit. And if we humans cannot be seen in such a way, life itself becomes a painful battle.

Second, we have come to view life in a divided or dualistic way. Dualism is as ancient as the Persians and the Greeks. Plato was perhaps the best example of this view. He called the body a prison, a ramshackle, dirty old jail which holds the pure spirit captive. Were it not for this incarceration in the body, the spirit would fly heavenward to God without a moment's pause. But, so this logic goes, the spirit must serve its time before it is released from its physical prison.

We Christians have incorporated this dualism into the very fabric of our piety and practice. We see the spirit as good and the body as evil. The dangers of this way of thinking are enormous. It has made us prisoners of our own self-hatred. We are walled off from doing that which we have been made to do. We are deprived of our senses. We are disembodied.

It is absolutely essential that we recover an appropriate understanding of the body. Otherwise it is all too easy to fall into one of the following traps:

• *"So spiritually minded, no earthly good."* If the world is cordoned off from Christian activity, then Christians become victims of overspiritualism. Our faith then becomes totally irrelevant to everyday life.

• *"Senseless" Christianity.* From this perspective the senses are seen only as means by which we can be led astray. One consequence of such a view is a lack of real joy. We may miss the joyous gifts God gives us in earthly life, and fail to share them with others as well.

● *"If it feels good, do it."* For those who simply seek pleasure, the body is the be-all and end-all, a means to unlimited good feelings. The flipside of such hedonism can be seen in those who spend their lives avoiding any and all pain. Such attitudes are especially dangerous for Christians because one cannot walk the way of the cross without pain.

● *Naive optimism.* A final trap is an optimistic and overly confident belief that human ingenuity can solve any problem that exists. This view maintains that given the right amount of creativity, work, technology, study, and capital, any difficulty can be overcome. Such a perspective often ignores the reality of sin in the world and fails to recognize the meaning of Christ's death and resurrection for human history.

The path to wholeness

If we are to avoid these traps we must regain an appreciation for the unity of our bodies and spirits. This is a difficult task, because we have been trained to distrust our bodies and not think of them as having anything to do with spirituality. But in the Scriptures we have a clear witness to the kind of unity and wholesomeness that we so desperately need.

The Bible bears witness to a personal wholeness which can be called "body spirituality." It seems ironic that we have to make a case for body spirituality, but that is exactly what this book seeks to do. We are not suggesting that "the way of the body" is to be chosen over "the way of the spirit." We would rather not make such distinctions. Each must be held together. Each must be followed. Each must be spoken in the same breath. That is exactly what we mean by body spirituality. And when the two are properly kept together, the result is a vibrant, full, and whole life.

The general opinion of most people is that the Bible has a dim view of the body. There are some passages that can be read in such a light. But the overwhelming witness of the Bible is that the body is good. Here are just a few of the passages which make up this total witness:

• *The creation stories.* "God saw everything that he had made, and behold, it was very good" (Gen. 1:31). God created our bodies and called them good. We need to remember that. People will tell us that because of the Fall our bodies are evil. But while sin and evil are real, they cannot destroy the essential goodness of God's creation. Our bodies certainly can become instruments of evil, especially when we choose to use them for evil. But in themselves they are good.

"The Lord God formed man of dust from the

ground, and breathed into his nostril the breath of life; and man became a living being" (Gen. 2:7). Such a marvelous image! It is an honor to be related so intimately with the earth, to the handiwork of God. We came from the earth and we will return to the earth. And into that earth God breathed the breath of life. A living being is one who possesses both a body *and* a spirit. There isn't one without the other.

• *Hosea and Gomer.* Throughout the Old Testament, body images are used to explain human beings, their life together, and their relationship to God. One example of this is the prophet Hosea and his difficult marriage with Gomer. Gomer had been repeatedly unfaithful to him. In spite of the pain he experienced, Hosea obeyed God by openly comparing Israel's unfaithfulness to the Lord with Gomer's unfaithfulness to him. God considered the powerful image of sexual infidelity to be an appropriate description of his people's rebellion against him.

• *A sensuous song.* The Song of Solomon provides a strong affirmation of physical and sexual life:

Behold, you are beautiful, my love,
behold, you are beautiful!
Your eyes are doves
behind your veil.
Your hair is like a flock of goats,

moving down the slopes of Gilead.
Your teeth are like a flock of shorn ewes
that have come up from the washing,
all of which bear twins,
and not one among them is bereaved.
Your lips are like a scarlet thread,
and your mouth is lovely.
Your cheeks are like halves of a pomegranate
behind your veil.
Your neck is like the tower of David,
built for an arsenal,
whereon hang a thousand bucklers,
all of them shields of warriors.
Your two breasts are like two fawns,
twins of a gazelle,
that feed among the lilies (4:1-5).

It is not surprising that this remarkable series of love songs was accepted as Scripture only after considerable debate. They have often been interpreted as a picture of the relationship between God and Israel and between Christ and the church. Whether merely beautiful and unabashed poems of love or analogies for God and his people, they are an important Old Testament witness to the blessings of physical existence in God's creation.

● *Paul's writings.* At times Paul seems to have been very direct in his criticism of bodily existence. His lists of sins, such as the one in Galatians 5, are

well-known: "Now the works of the flesh are plain: fornication, impurity, licentiousness, idolatry, sorcery, enmity, strife, jealousy, anger, selfishness, dissension, party spirit, envy, drunkenness, carousing, and the like." A close examination of this list reveals that only five of these "works of the flesh" are bodily in nature. *The other ten are "spiritual" sins.* If Paul was "against the body," as some people charge, then he was "against the spirit" even more! For Paul, "the flesh" is not identical with the body. It is rather that part of human beings which is at enmity with God.

In 1 Corinthians 7 Paul champions celibacy and seems to disparage sexuality and the body. But two things need to be noted about that chapter. First, Paul believed (as many early Christians did) that Jesus would return very soon. In the light of his imminent return, everything else (family, marriage, work, and so forth) was of lesser importance. Anything which might distract a believer's attention from this event was undesirable. Paul's counsel to Christians was therefore to remain as they were. They should not make any changes in their lives which might distract them from the coming of the Lord. He counseled those who were single not to marry, and he counseled those who were married to remain married. He was more interested in stability than in celibacy.

Second, 1 Corinthians 7 is not a blanket condemnation. Instead, it is a selective warning about misuses of the body. Apparently at that time there was a great deal of dualistic thinking in Corinth. The spirit was seen as most important, while the body was viewed as a prison or as the spirit's dull-witted companion. What one did with one's body didn't matter, some said, because the body wasn't real, eternal, or essential. This attitude resulted in an "anything goes" hedonism which Paul had to battle constantly. Our negative reading of Paul may be a result of hearing his warnings apart from the problems to which they were addressed.

In Romans 12 Paul says, "I appeal to you therefore, brethren, by the mercies of God, to present your *bodies* as a living sacrifice, holy and acceptable to God, which is your *spiritual* worship" (italics added). Making our bodies a living sacrifice means offering them each day as a treasure that would be acceptable to God. In doing so, Paul informs us, we will be worshiping God. Worship—truly spiritual worship—involves respecting and caring for the body. An active, body-centered life is what the Christian faith is all about. That is Christian spirituality. That is body spirituality. If offering one's whole body is spiritual, then isn't it a spiritual thing to involve one's whole body in worship? Couldn't work on behalf of a just political cause be seen as a spiritual act? If we take Paul seriously, the old distinctions between sacred and secular, religious and profane cannot be so glibly made.

Paul didn't see the body as a prison, but as the temple of the Holy Spirit (1 Cor. 3:16). He would not have us hide or hate our bodies. Rather, we are to honor Christ in them (Phil. 1:20). Paul's benediction to the church at Thessalonica should perhaps become ours as well:

May the God of peace himself sanctify you wholly; and may your spirit and soul and body be kept sound and blameless at the coming of our Lord Jesus Christ (1 Thess. 5:23).

In addition to the many biblical passages which bear witness to God's intention of wholeness for our lives, the Bible provides us with some powerful *signs* or *sacraments* of wholeness:

● *Circumcision: an unlikely symbol.* The importance of circumcision to the people of Israel cannot be overestimated. Unlike the Temple, circumcision was a sign of God's covenant which could not be destroyed. Even in Egyptian servitude and Babylonian exile, circumcision remained a clear sign of Israel's relationship with God. And no matter how we try to avoid it, circumcision is a surgical act performed on the penis. How utterly physical! How amazingly graphic! In this act we can see the natural way the Old Testament associates the physical with the spiritual. It sees no artificial distinction between the two.

● *Baptism.* Jesus commanded his followers to baptize disciples. Like circumcision, Baptism is a very physical act which includes a spiritual dimension. For Christians, this act of "drowning" is closely connected with the death of one's old sinful self and the beginning of new life in Christ.

• *The Lord's Supper.* The Lord's Supper is another powerful biblical symbol of the unity of the physical and the spiritual. Those who eat the bread and drink the wine of Holy Communion in faith encounter the risen Christ and are strengthened in their Christian lives.

• *Christ's incarnation.* "And the Word became flesh and dwelt among us, full of grace and truth" (John 1:14). There is no more positive affirmation of our physical existence than the Word becoming flesh in Jesus Christ. Christ entered the world and redeemed the irredeemable. He gave wholeness to the fragmented and united the separated. The incarnation is God's radical and ultimate yes to human beings in their totality. And as followers of Jesus, the in-the-flesh God, we are empowered by his Spirit in our bodies. We are sent into the world to help transform it by God's presence.

• *The resurrection of the dead.* Not only does God say yes to our physical existence, but in Christ he leads us into a future physical existence with him. Christ's resurrection was no spiritualistic victory, but the physical raising of Jesus' whole person from death by the power of God. And because we are united with Christ's death and resurrection through Bap-

tism, we trust that we will one day join him in a kind
of physical existence that is even more exciting than
the one we now know.

Finding reconciliation

We cannot live with one foot in "heaven" and the
other on this worldly "banana peel." We cannot so
easily divide life that way. The existence we share
now is both physical and spiritual in nature. There
cannot be one without the other. Our bodies are our
pathways into the world. They release us into the
sunlight of all creation. They are the doors that open
us to God's manifold presence in the world. Our
bodies are not shameful, unholy captors of our spirits.
Rather than distancing us from God, they bring us
closer.

Our senses of sight, sound, taste, smell, and touch
are our bodies in conversation with the world around
us. Our spirits would exist in a vacuous nothingness
without our bodies. They would miss the warming
sun, the smell of freshly baked bread, and the per-
spiration of play. Through our bodies we experience
the treasures of God's creation. And through our
spirits we sense the presence of God in these treasures. Through our senses we are literally touched
by God. We see the Bible's pages. We hear music,
prayer, and preaching. We smell and taste the bread
and wine of the Lord's Supper. We feel the loving

hugs of Christian brothers and sisters. Our bodies are
the means by which we know God.

In this book we will be exploring our spiritual relationship with God through some very physical
things: prayer, food, movement, and play. We are
convinced that by building on the Bible's witness
to human wholeness, each of us can grow closer to
ourselves, God, creation, and others. As we become
more aware and appreciative of the physical gifts
that God has given us, we can learn to experience
our true unity as God's creatures.

Experiences and exercises

1. What negative attitudes do you have toward
your body? How do these attitudes affect your relationship with God?

2. Review the "traps" on pp. 30-31. Have you
lapsed into any of these? How might you cure this
imbalance?

3. What do you think of when you hear the phrase,
"body spirituality"? What are some ways that you
relate to God through your physical existence?

4. Find some additional Bible passages that speak
of spiritual and physical wholeness.

2

The Body
and Prayer

Prayer is at the very heart of all Christian life. Yet
many of us find it hard to pray. We are often uncomfortable with formal prayers, and have trouble
praying on our own. We have known prayer only as
those moments when we cease what we're doing,
fold our hands, close our eyes, bow our heads, speak
directly to God, and then close with a reverent
"amen." There can be quite a distance between such
prayers and our daily lives. As a result, we may
either just go through the motions or else give up
such prayers altogether.

Most prayers have the same basic elements. Traditional forms of prayer can be very helpful, but if our
experience is limited to them, we may find that our
growth in prayer is restricted.

● *Most prayers are monologs*. We say our piece and await God's response. God is somewhere "out there," and prayer is our way of getting his attention. But if prayer is truly communication with God, then it must be a two-way street. Not only do we need to talk to God, we also need to listen to God.

● *Most prayers are mental*. They are products of our intellects. But if prayer reflects our whole relationship with God, then it must include *all* of us: minds, bodies, and spirits. We must communicate with God as whole persons.

● *Most prayers are conscious*. We think we must be alert, undistracted, solemn, and in control. But we don't always know exactly what the particular needs of a situation are and what response from God would be best. We need to bring the rest of ourselves to God as well: scattered thoughts, semiconscious images, mixed feelings, and irrelevant utterances.

● *Most prayers are verbal*. Whether spoken aloud or in our minds, our prayers usually take the shape of the spoken, verbalized word. We think them through. And yet our innermost urgings and yearnings cannot always be clearly articulated. These, too, are a part of prayer.

● *Most prayers are systematic*. They have predictable introductions, conclusions, vocabulary, and content. But an insistence on such forms for *every*

prayer puts a barrier between us and God. Sometimes our deepest needs need to be expressed spon-
taneously and in novel ways.

We need expanded horizons in our understanding
of prayer. Sometimes prayer is explicit and articulate,
conforming to the traditional pattern. But at other
times it includes those inarticulate moments, those
pains and passions so deep that the spirit must pray
for us and through us. Prayer includes our leaping
hearts, confused minds, and tumultous bodies. It is
both spiritual *and* physical.

We pray whether we intend to or not. Our very
lives are expressions of our deepest commitments,
and our whole existence is really one continuous
prayer. Prayer is like breathing, a constant inhalation
and exhalation of the spirit. It is a tide which ebbs
and flows. Just as there is no time in which we do
not breathe, so there is no moment when we are not
in communication with God.

When we see prayer in this broad sense, we can
find a way out of our false distinctions between the
physical and the spiritual. We can learn to bring all
of ourselves to God in a variety of ways. As whole
persons, we can involve our minds, bodies, and
spirits in a joyous, daily relationship with God. And
our experiences of prayer in all its many forms will
breathe new life into our more formal and struc-
tured times of prayer.

What is meditation?

One helpful way to broaden our prayer life is through meditation. When most people hear the word *meditation,* they immediately think of Eastern religions or their Western adaptations such as Transcendental Meditation. Most do not realize that meditation has been part of the Christian tradition for centuries. Christian meditative practices reached a peak during the Middle Ages, although they are seeing a modest revival today.

Meditation simply means being "in the middle" of something. One can be in the middle of a conversation with God, solitude, or nature. Since there are so many misunderstandings about what meditation actually is, we will begin by saying what it is *not.*

• *Meditation is not necessarily religious.* There is the potential for meditation to become a cult of its own. But this potential is no greater than that in many political parties, corporations, or other organizations.

• *Meditation is not innately demonic or evil.* The Scriptures tell us that "nothing is unclean in itself" (Rom. 14:14). It is what one *intends* or *does* with something that is either demonic or holy. Meditation is no more demonic than playing softball. As a tool or technique, it is neutral. The person using it is the one who makes it what it is.

• *Meditation is not a cure-all.* Like anything that

is new and exciting in our lives, we tend to inflate the importance of it. While we celebrate the benefits which meditation can bring, we realize that it has its limitations. It cannot change an unhappy marriage or oppressive working conditions. It cannot eliminate the starvation and deprivation which are experienced by the poor in our world.

• *Meditation is not simply a technique for coping with pressure.* It is misused when it is merely a method to make our pains go away. Many Westerners have welcomed with open arms the Eastern idea that pain and suffering are actually unreal and are therefore to be ignored and avoided. Meditation can help change our feelings about a problem, but its deeper causes will remain unaffected until we face them head-on.

Why meditate?

There are many reasons why meditation can be a helpful part of one's Christian life. Here are a few:

• *Listening to God.* Through meditation our sensitivities can be sharpened to receive God's presence and word for us. We can become more receptive to seeing the face of Christ in another's eyes. We can hear God's voice in our own creative pursuits day by day. Through meditation we can cultivate our senses to be more keenly alert to the "still small voice" of God which is not heard by most people.

● *Understanding ourselves.* Like a very sensitive camera, meditation can reveal things about us that we often do not see. When we sit silently for a few moments and clear our minds, we frequently come face-to-face with our inner selves. We discover that we are a mixture of good and evil, joy and sadness, boldness and fear. And in that confrontation we can also decide who we want to become.

● *Understanding others.* By identifying with other people through meditation, we can come to a fuller awareness of lives beyond our own. Our sensitivities to others can be refined. We can perceive those things in peoples' lives which are subtly camouflaged but in acute need of our concern. By meditating on the injustices in other peoples' lives we can, in an admittedly vicarious way, experience a small portion of their pain. Our awareness of someone else's need can become so vivid that inaction is more painful than the fear of action.

● *A call to action.* As we become more open to messages about ourselves, others, and God, we often experience a strangely exciting sense of calm. We feel whole, tranquil, and at one with the world. But then the peace disappears. We are back to our normal lives, no longer experiencing peace but still believing that all is well. Plainly, it is not. Nor was it during our momentary sense of wholeness. Such experiences are rather lures for us, clues to the future. They speak not of what is but of what will be. Having re-

ceived a foretaste of God's arrival and the heavenly
banquet that will follow, we are assigned the task of
preparing the world for him. Our experiences of
wholeness call us to action, both in proclaiming the
gospel to all people and in caring for their present
needs. We are called into study, prayer, and action.

• *Dealing with sudden changes.* There are circumstances in which our lives seem out of control and
we feel severely threatened. We may lose a companion or a spouse. We may lose a job. An accident
may handicap us for life. Whatever the crisis, it is
necessary to rebuild ourselves physically and spiritually. Meditation can be an excellent way to reduce
emotional or physical pain which we cannot bear.
It can offer us a "bridge over troubled waters" which
might keep us from drowning. When meditation is
part of a larger solution in such circumstances, we
commend its use.

• *Dealing with long-term changes.* There are other
changes which affect us over a long period of time.
Meditation can then be a valuable means of adjustment. For example, the diets and attendant habits
which most of us have are unhealthy and overly
consumptive of the world's food resources. We can
decide to change, but we may find that our old patterns are difficult to break. During the time it takes
to satisfactorily modify those habits, meditation can
be an invaluable asset. It can give strength to with-
stand the inevitable physical and emotional discom-

fort. It can awaken patience to endure and new resolve when we stray.

Trying it out

If you are unfamiliar with meditation, what follows
may help you get started. Once you have become
comfortable with the discipline, you will discover
that you will create your own style and timing. You
will also be able to design and construct your own
meditative journeys. In your early attempts it may
be easier to meditate with no one else around to interrupt you or make it difficult to relax. You may,
however, find it difficult to remember the various
steps and still meditate. If you find that to be a
problem, perhaps a friend or spouse could guide you.
You should not be overly concerned if, in the early
stages of your learning, you find yourself falling
asleep. This happens quite often.

Two different styles of meditation are described in
the following pages. The first is a more traditional
sort in which the meditator is in a seated or lying
posture and remains immobile throughout the meditation. This is stationary or seated meditation. The
second type is called movement meditation, and involves some kind of physical activity.

Before you begin either kind of meditation, you
should consider a few basic suggestions. They will
facilitate and deepen your meditative experience:

● *Take plenty of time.* A minimum of 10-15 minutes should be allowed for stationary meditation and 20-30 minutes for movement meditation. Inexperienced meditators will need even more time. Be aware that rushing through meditation will diminish its effect.

● *Select a conducive environment.* This is particularly important for stationary meditation. Too many distractions may detract from the experience. Do not let this prevent you from meditating, however. Your environment can be overcome by accepting it into your meditation. We will describe how this can be done in stationary meditation. In movement meditation, your environment can be of almost any sort.

● *Dress appropriately.* Wear loose-fitting, comfortable clothes that don't restrict your body or distract your attention.

● *Warm up beforehand.* A few relaxation techniques and stretching exercises will help prepare you. Again, take your time. The quality of your preparation will affect the richness of your meditative experience. For example, try the following relaxation exercise: Begin with your head and shoulders. Slowly tighten your neck and shoulder muscles. When they are as tight as you want them to be, hold them for three counts and then release them. Continue doing this with various muscle groups all the way down to your toes. Keep your breathing smooth and deep.

Finally, let all your muscles become lose. Imagine them to be simply dangling from your bones, sagging in complete relaxation, as though they would fall off if not for your skin and ligaments. After such stretching and relaxing you will be ready for meditation.

Stationary meditation

Assume a posture that is comfortable for you. It may be in your favorite easy chair, sitting on a soft carpet, or lying down. Balance your center of gravity. If your body weight is not balanced and evenly distributed, you may grow uncomfortable. Once you are set, begin to breathe steadily and ever more deeply. Take just a few moments to focus on that. Then allow your eyelids to drop. Don't force them shut. That only creates tension. Allow them to close as much as feels comfortable. If they become completely closed, that's fine. If not, you will be aware that your vision is cloudy. Focus on nothing specific, but dreamily take everything in, not moving your eyes at all.

Now bring your attention back to your breathing. Each breath goes deeper and deeper into your lungs. Don't force it. Each breath will deepen on its own. Breathe in as far as is comfortable. Let your exhaled breath rush out on its own. It does not need to be forced. Keep the breathing regular. Be aware of the transition point between inhalation and exhalation.

Focus on that. Concentrate on rounding off the transitions. Guide and measure your breathing so that you cannot tell when inhalation becomes exhalation or exhalation turns to inhalation. If your breathing is choppy and the transitions are swift and sharp, it is too shallow and irregular. Round it off. Deepen it. Breathe deeply and steadily.

Now direct your attention to your environment. Listen to the sounds around you. Smell the smells. Feel the temperature, the movements of air as it passes over the exposed parts of your skin. Be aware of outside sounds: cars, children playing, background music. Accept them. Don't edit or judge your sensations. Just accept them, listen to them, and let them pass through your consciousness. Do the same with the aromas that you become aware of. Let the sensations on your flesh also come to your awareness. Let them come and go as they will. Neither dwell overly long on them nor try to push them out of your field of awareness. Accept them. Take them into yourself. Let them pass just as freely as they came. Be patient. Take your time. Breathe deeply.

As you feel more open to yourself and accepting of your surroundings, you may focus your awareness on your body. Begin with your feet. Feel your feet from the inside as well as the outside. Be aware of where the pressure points are. Where is there tension? Feel the shoe, carpeting, grass, or sheet that touches them. Don't push these sensations away, even the tense or

constricting ones. Stay with them. Accept them. Let
them be. Feel the bottoms of your feet. What does
it feel like in the area between your toes? Breathe
deeply. Breathe smoothly. Breathe patiently.

Now glide your attention slowly up your legs.
Again feel the areas of tension, where your garments
touch and hang. Feel subtle tickles here and there.
Don't force them away. Just experience them. Become aware of your knees, the back as well as the
front. Feel the places on your body that are most
firmly in contact with the ground. Sense your bones
and muscles. Notice the pulsations in your muscles.
Notice how they match rhythm with the beating
of your heart. When you are ready, move your awareness to your hips, abdomen, and lower back. Focus
your attention on each of those areas respectively.
Give time to experience them fully. Notice the activity. Follow it as it moves. Don't evaluate or judge
these sensations. There is no need to interpret them.
Just experience them.

Move your awareness slowly up your back. As you
do, recognize how strongly, steadily, and silently
your muscles gird and support your spine. If you are
lying on your back, notice that even in relaxation
those muscles have a firmness to them. Note how
your chest rises and subsides with each breath you
take. Breathe smoothly and deeply. Inhale. Exhale.
Feel your lungs fill with new air. They billow out,
brightly and joyously. Let them draw out of you the

shadows, grit, and congestion within. As you exhale, watch the internal pollution swiftly rush away with your breath, easily, deeply. Breathe.

Concentrate on your heart for awhile. Can you feel its beat? Notice your pulse as it surges through other parts of your body, especially the sides of your neck, your fingertips, and your legs. Observe how your entire body subtly pulsates in rhythm, steadily, regularly, unceasingly. If parts of your body are touching or resting on each other, feel how the point of contact matches your heart's beating. Focus your attention on your fingers. Feel how your finger muscles, joints, and flesh curl when they are relaxed. Feel the skin between your fingers. Its sense of touch is keen. Continue on up from your elbows to your shoulders and the base of your neck. Feel how firm and confident the muscles are which support your head.

When you are ready, move your awareness to your head. Feel where your hair brushes your collar, the back of your head, your ears, and your forehead. Occasionally spots on your head will tickle or itch. Feel the irritation, but don't scratch. Allow them to be, and they will pass. Note how the skin on your forehead, cheeks, and chin is firm yet relaxed. Sense the air as it wafts across your face. Your lips are tightly sealed and tingle. The air caresses the inside of your nostrils as you breathe in and out.

Your eyelids delicately but warmly protect the

surface of your eyes. You see their backside. In the light darkness you perceive some areas as darker than others. Perhaps a dust particle floats silently across. Your vision deepens and deepens. You slowly begin to see with your mind's eye. You notice colors: reds, blues, yellows brightening into white, or fathoms of darkness. Images grow and fade. Faces may suddenly flash. Thoughts grow. Scenes appear from the past. Fantasies dance and play. Quickly they come and quickly they go. Some flash. Some are fuzzy. One image changes shape to form an altogether different one. Unusual and fascinating stories play themselves out before your mind's eye. Don't try to remold or reshape them. Don't direct, guide, or control them. Don't work at getting rid of them. Don't try to hold onto them. Let them come and go as they will. Let them flow. Some will be fleeting. Others will stay for awhile. You don't have to put them in order or make sense out of them. Just observe and accept them. They will move on their own accord. They are a part of you, part of your past and future. Observe. Appreciate. Accept.

Continue to observe your breathing. It flows steadily, full and smooth. You may sense you are part of something larger. Your environment is one awesome organism, and you live in harmony with it. You may even sense that the air is breathing *you,* nurturing and caring for you.

Continue sensing and experiencing until it seems

appropriate to begin ending the meditation. Go easily. There is no need to be abrupt. Patiently collect yourself. Gradually focus your breathing and thoughts. When the time feels right, allow your eyes to open. They may open very slowly. Slowly light will penetrate your foggy vision. You will be calmed and relaxed. When you are fully and vividly aware, you have completed your meditation. Allow the feelings and insights from the experience to guide you through the remainder of your day.

Movement meditation

Movement meditation aims at wholeness by involving the body more directly. The particular movement form could be one of many different types: aerobic dance, bicycling, swimming, walking, or jogging. The illustrations and examples we give here come from our own jogging experience. But with a few modifications they would fit other activities as well. They will, however, work most effectively with those activities that are habitual, methodical, solitary, and noncompetitive.

Careful selection of your environment is important for movement meditation. In particular you need to be concerned about personal safety. For bicycling and jogging, traffic is an obvious danger. Yet even aerobic dance in your own living room can be dangerous. Loose electrical cords, sharp corners on furniture, and low-hanging lights all need to be considered. Plan ahead to remove such distractions. Nurture a sense of freedom within by carefully selecting your environment. Then prepare yourself for deep and free involvement in meditation.

As you begin your movement meditation, you may find the following suggestions helpful:

• *Begin slowly.* After some warm-up stretching and perhaps some brief stationary meditation, begin your activity. Move slowly at first. Allow time for the flow of blood to catch up with your increased body effort. Breathe deeply and slowly, so that oxygen and needed blood circulation can ease possible muscle tightness. Try to keep your breathing regular and deep throughout. In the early minutes of jogging, go easily. Note the tension areas and allow them to loosen. Sometimes this may require stopping and doing a little extra stretching in those particular areas. For muscle groups in the arms and shoulders, a three to five second contraction of the tense areas followed by relaxation is helpful. Scan your entire body for other areas of tension. By heeding signs of tension early you will avoid unnecessary distraction, discomfort, or even injury.

• *Pace yourself.* A useful rule of thumb about pacing is, you are running too fast if you can't carry on a normal conversation with someone alongside you. If you are breathless and can only speak short, choppy sentences, you should slow down. Once you begin perspiring you may increase your speed slightly. Start matching the rhythm of your leg and arm movements with your breathing. It may be difficult at first, but with practice you'll discover there is a very natural relationship between your movement and your breathing. For some, establishing a mental cadence is helpful. For example, for each inhalation (or exhalation) there will be four footfalls. For a complete breathing cycle there will be eight footfalls. Another helpful technique is to recite a poem or sing a favorite tune in rhythm. It *is* possible for all parts of your body to work as one—smoothly and efficiently.

• *Practice internal imagery.* When you are well into a run, try visualizing the earth as revolving on its axis at the same speed and in the opposite direction as you are running. Then imagine that the only energy required of you is to lift your feet so that the world may turn beneath you. In effect, you remain stationary while the world does the turning. Or envision yourself as a sleek, graceful animal such as a gazelle or a cheetah, gliding and bounding across the land. The variety of images available for use are limited only by your imagination. Try them out. Experiment. Discover how they enrich your meditation.

• *Practice external imagery.* In addition to your internal images, be aware of the external world as a rich resource. As you run, notice early morning

breakfast smells, children in playgrounds, birds chat-
tering, or oddly sculpted trees. Contemplate that
cluster of flowers that seems to glow with an aura
of bright colors. Gaze at the clouds floating on the
horizon. Listen closely to the trees as they breathe.

• *Pray consciously.* A daily jog can be an excellent time for offering conscious prayers to God. They
may be joyous or sad, full of praise, lament, confes-
sion, petition, or thanksgiving. Prayer while running
can be an opportunity to offer your whole self to
God, undistracted and uncluttered by other thoughts
or concerns. The rigors of a hard run force frankness,
open and honest conversation with God. A repeated
word or phrase may also be added to your running
rhythm. The Jesus Prayer ("Jesus, Son of God,
have mercy on me") or the Kyrie ("Lord have mercy, Christ have mercy") can be especially meaningful if recited repetitively to the rhythm of your run.
Some people visualize the names and faces of those
they love. It is amazing how often one can enter
movement meditation with anxiety, dread, sadness,
or a penitent attitude and conclude it with a sense
of hope, love, and a forgiving spirit!

• *Be aware.* As you run, frequently monitor your
breathing, tension areas, and rhythm. On those days
when everything is at peak efficiency, a profound
appreciation for life may unexpectedly rush over you.
You may feel at one with yourself and the universe.
Such experiences cannot be guaranteed. They are

spontaneous and unpredictable. But neither should you be overwhelmed by them if they come. Be alert and sensitive, and you will no doubt experience a bit of what it means to be part of God's good creation!

Experiences and exercises

1. Record where, how, when, and in what postures you pray or meditate. Why do you do it that way? What new ways might you try?

2. This week try out a new way of praying. Here are some suggestions:

- put movements of prayer to music;
- sit, run, swim, or bike, with the activity being an expression of prayer;
- close your eyes and see colors and configurations in your mind's eye (with as few words as possible); let God interpret this prayer in his own way.

3

The Body and Food

Many years ago the German philosopher Ludwig Feuerbach remarked, "We are what we eat." The truth of that statement is incontestable. We see what our bodies have become, and we know what we've eaten to get there.

Eating reveals a lot about us. It speaks of our values (from TV dinners to gourmet meals), our habits (from fasting to feasting), and our idiosyncrasies (from peanut butter and banana sandwiches to escargot). The eating habits of most of us reveal some disturbing things. We overeat, even though we know better. We eat far too much grain-fed animal protein. We consume too much sugar, salt, and fat—known contributors to cavities, hypertension, and heart disease. We eat large amounts of additives that have been shown to cause cancer. We eat too many processed foods, even though much of their nutritive value has been lost. And then we overcook our food and lose much of the food value which remains. Often our food is simply an afterthought, a bother, or an interruption. We take little time to prepare it or enjoy it.

One of the most poignant statements about nutrition in America is made every day behind restaurants, grocery stores, and homes. The garbage cans in these places contain much good food, food people have left on their plates or which may be one day past the approved health level. So often we dispose of food because we bought too much, didn't plan our meals carefully, or simply because it is convenient to throw it away. American garbage pails contain better food than that eaten by the majority of the world's population. Yet it's hard for us to appreciate this nutritional waste because our food is so plentiful and so cheap. In many parts of the world the majority of a worker's pay goes toward food. In parts of Africa 90% goes toward purchasing foodstuffs. Yet in America, often only 20% to 30% of our income goes toward this basic need. While we fret over the amount we eat, we should be just as concerned about what we do *not* eat—and instead throw away.

Nutrition: more than what we eat

Nutrition is what we eat, but it is far more than

that. It is also *how* we eat, *where* we eat, *when* we eat, *why* we eat, and *with whom* we eat. All these physical aspects of eating have their spiritual aspects as well. The manner in which we eat the Creator's good gifts and the spirit in which we view nutrition say a great deal about our own body spirituality.

• *How we eat.* Our eating style is generally on the run, in a hurry, and gulping as we go. It's such a longstanding habit that we are hardly aware it is happening. This was illustrated recently by a humorous incident during dinner. Midway through a community meal it became apparent that everyone was in a terrible hurry. It seemed like an old-time movie. So the diners consciously slowed down. But before long they were once again gobbling down their food like barnyard animals. Suddenly it dawned on them what was happening. Coming from the next room, blasting forth from the radio, was a fast ragtime piece by Scott Joplin. No wonder they were hurrying! Our surroundings have a great influence on how we eat.

We also need to look at how we prepare our food. There are other ways of cooking besides boiling, baking, and broiling. We need to learn to prepare our food with a view toward preserving its food value, whether we steam it, stew it, stir-fry it, or ·eat it raw. How we prepare our food is partially a result of our attitude. Too often we literally throw it together. One Asian writer has commented that

we Americans, who are so future-oriented, need to focus on the present. For example, instead of peeling an orange just to get the slices, he suggests that sometime we just peel it for the sake of peeling. We can deepen our nutritional consciousness by concentrating on the act of preparing food itself.

Finally, we need to look at how we serve our food. Again it is a question of style and attitude. Do you remember the comic strip in the Sunday paper called "The Better Half," especially the perennial episodes at Bert's Beanery? Bert had a real knack for making everything he cooked taste like beans. The way we serve food can make even the best-tasting ingredients come out tasting like Bert's beans.

• *Where we eat.* Make a list sometime of where you eat. You may find that you eat in the strangest places. We frequent fast-food outlets, and as a result end up eating in our cars. Eating is one of the most pleasurable events in life. Yet many of us eat while driving down the road. The cost is high in terms of lack of enjoyment, tension, and poor health. Of course there is no one "spiritual" place to eat. Any place will do. But the spirit we bring to our eating should enable us to experience thankfulness, health, and love.

When we buy food, we often shop automatically at a supermarket, even though we know the prices are higher because of overprocessing, advertising, and packaging. But there are other choices. There are small grocery stores, farmers' markets, and co-ops. And best of all, we can grow our *own* food. There *are* alternatives to supermarkets, but we need to exercise our options and support them.

• *When we eat.* How much of your eating is governed by the clock rather than your stomach? When sitting in a big office with a clock on the wall, magic happens at noon every day as stomachs still half-full from breakfast are told it's time to eat again. After years of such conditioning one doesn't even need a clock anymore. It all becomes internalized, and our heads tell our stomachs to feel empty. Perhaps the strangest thing about this clock-watching syndrome is that the times we are assigned for eating don't really fit our modern schedules. The noon lunch is a remnant of our rural past. Farmers were up before dawn doing chores. They came in for breakfast very early, around 6:00 A.M. Then they went back into the fields to work til noon. They broke for a small lunch and a rest to avoid the heat of the day. Even though most of us today don't rise as early or work as hard physically, we eat lunch at noon anyway, hungry or not. And to this meal, rushed as it is, we often add a quick drink or two.

If our schedule isn't as regular as most, it probably still follows a pattern. We eat at certain times of the day just to pass or fill time, to overcome boredom or frustration. Too often we fill an already over-filled stomach because of another kind of empty space in our lives. Take time to reflect on when you eat. A helpful way to explore this is to not eat at all for a period of time—to fast. As Jesus and many of the church's great teachers have recognized, nutrition involves not only celebrative feasts but also prayerful fasts. Fast and pray. The awareness of when you eat and do not eat will lead to a deepened, more spiritual sense of nutrition.

• *Why we eat.* Not only does the clock rule our stomachs, but our work and business often dictate our nutritional patterns. Many people do their business over a meal. Mealtime and food become a background for other concerns. At times, in order to impress a customer or client, the richest, most expensive, and least nutritious items are selected. In addition to causing obesity and alcoholism, such a style of eating also makes family meals seem prosaic. Meals can be a part of work, but they can also be an interruption from work. A work break, rather than being rest and recreation, becomes an excuse to snack on cookies, donuts, and junk food available in ever-present food machines. Eating is often a very accurate emotional barometer. If we are upset or nervous or worried, we eat. If we feel we have been mistreated, we will at least feed ourselves well.

Why do we eat? Obviously we must eat if we don't want to die. But our motivation to eat can be celebration of God's goodness rather than compulsion born of boredom. At a Samaritan well Jesus

spoke of spiritual food and drink to a woman who was too concerned with the physical part of life. Today, in our haste to separate the physical aspect of eating from our spiritual lives, Jesus may be calling us back to wholeness and refreshment.

• *With whom we eat.* When most of us were growing up, the evening meal was a special family time. Now dinner is often announced by a note on the refrigerator door indicating on which shelf to look. With school schedules, more women working outside the home, and increased travel, the occasions for meals together (let alone nutritious ones) are becoming few and far between. And if a balanced, wholesome meal is not provided at home, it may not be provided at all. Eating is something to do with others, together. It is a time to share. We need to seek ways to make our mealtimes healthy and joyful communal experiences.

It is true that many people today find themselves eating alone. But such eating need not be lonely or haphazard. Often a silent, prayerful meal can be the richest of spiritual experiences. Christian monastics learned this long ago. And there is no reason why a solitary meal needs to be nutritionally deficient. One of the reasons we find it difficult to cook for just ourselves is that we are accustomed to over-elaborate preparation. A meal need not be hours in the making in order to be healthy and good.

Nutrition that is life-giving and nurturing for our

bodies is more than just what we eat. Total nutrition involves not only our bodies, but our whole beings.

Four visions of nutrition

A friend once said that people change for two reasons: either they are frightened by a nightmare or they are drawn toward a new vision. So far this chapter has looked more like the former than the latter. What follows are four hopeful visions of a better nutritional future.

• *Health and cure.* In our culture, "health" is usually determined by an annual checkup. At such a checkup, average health is determined by comparison with other Americans. Unfortunately, the general level of health among American citizens is not very high. According to global health studies, America ranks in the second one-third. Further, health is defined by American doctors, who unfortunately know far more about disease than about health. Most doctors also know very little about nutrition. For many, one course in medical school is the extent of their nutritional learning. Yet both increasing scientific evidence and common sense tell us that nutrition plays a central role in health. Good nutrition is the very cornerstone of the prevention and cure of disease as well as the maintenance of not just average health, but high-level wellness.

A careful, nutritious, and tasty diet is a key to

health, and costs far less than radical medical treatment for a neglected or abused body. Too often we provide more preventive care for our automobiles or other machinery than we do for our bodies. Part of the problem is ignorance and part is laziness. Reeducation, practice, and patience are needed ingredients in putting together a new, simple, and nutritious diet.

Too often we think God works miracles only in extraordinary ways. But the best way God interacts with his creation may be the most obvious. God's will is done when we humans wisely use those natural gifts he has given us. God is present for us in the good and holy things of life like bread and wine, cheese and vegetables, herbs and spices.

• *Politics and change.* Food is a political issue. A good example is the practice of vegetarianism. Note how many vegetarians are considered to be suspicious radicals by their meat-eating counterparts. Notice, too, how some vegetarians turn their eating habits into a brand of elitism. Why are people and powers so threatened and defensive if food is not a political issue?

In the world of food, many political decisions are made, and most of these are made *for* you. Look once more at what, where, why, and when you eat. We all have some freedom of choice in these matters. But on closer inspection, you will discover that your options are more limited than you might have thought. On a lunch break, unless you bring your own food, it's unlikely that you will have much choice in the matter of what you eat. Your options are very limited. How about your purchase of foodstuffs? Despite an abundance of stores, the varieties of food are the same. Unless you are quite creative and willing to undergo some inconvenience, you have to buy from a large supermarket. If you look there to buy fresh, tasty food without additives, you may find yourself limited to the produce section.

In order to have some freedom of choice concerning our food, we must act. We must take charge and seek change. Change does not happen by itself. Through our eating habits we can affect the politics of food for good or ill. And as Christians it is vital that we involve ourselves directly in the formation of public food policies so that the decisions concerning production and distribution best meet the needs of all people.

 • *Happiness and care.* As human beings we have basic needs. In addition to food and shelter we need to be loved and cared for. Without love, most of us would not only die emotionally, but physically as well. When we are not cared for or about, we would just as soon be dead. We experience love and care most significantly with our families, especially at mealtimes. For most of us, our memories of growing up include meals as being almost synonymous with family. In spite of arguments and conflicts, we have many positive and warm memories from family meals. Mealtimes are, at their best, sacred gatherings where people come together to share, laugh, eat, cry, and be supported.

It should not surprise us that the Bible is full of such meals and feasts. Feasts to welcome a son home, to celebrate a wedding, to share in the bounty of a harvest. There were come-as-you-are affairs like the feeding of the 5000 or the eating of grain while strolling through the fields. At Jesus' Last Supper with his disciples, the breaking of bread and the sharing of the cup made Jesus' love and care and forgiveness present once again. And in his appearance to two disciples after his death, Jesus was not recognized until "the breaking of the bread" (Luke 24: 35).

Jesus used such feasts to describe what the kingdom of God was like. Earthly feasts and banquets were beautiful images for the celebration, excitement, enjoyment, and plenty of God's heavenly table, where all his people would gather. The biblical writers repeatedly emphasized the communal nature of eating. It is something we all must do, something which naturally evokes thanksgiving for God's good gifts. The feast or banquet is a symbol passed on to our generation in order that we may continue to feed not only our bodies, but also our hungry spirits.

The Lord's Supper is all too frequently seen as an extraordinary occurrence. Granted, it is not just another banquet. But the capital letters and the holy aspects of Communion may raise this wonderfully down-to-earth experience of God right out of reach and sight. God sent a physical Messiah and Jesus instituted a physical meal so that we could see and touch and experience God's love. Can't we also broaden our understanding of everyday meals in this light? With such a transformed vision of eating, we may discover Christ not only in the breaking of the bread, but also in all who gather around our family table, our church table, and the global table of God.

• *Enjoyment and celebration.* Too often, eating is a bland experience for us. This is usually because there is little variety in our diet. It's hard to compete with food professionals, and it's especially difficult for one person to always be burdened with the responsibility of food preparation. Eating involves all of our senses. And because they are all involved, we should experience enjoyment. Try some of the following suggestions to help wake up your senses as you eat: *taste:* go beyond salt and pepper; try some of the herbs and spices used in international cooking; *touch:* instead of just a knife and fork, try chopsticks or a fingerfood extravaganza; *smell:* a few minutes of food scents just before mealtime are wonderful; it is even more grand to have that all-day-long smell of food cooking; *sights:* rather than plastic wrappers and aluminum foil, try an artistic arrangement of colors which complement and entice; *sounds:* replace

the clamor of a restaurant or the automobile exhaust of a drive-in with the bubbling of stews or the siz-zling of sauté.

A new appreciation for the experience of meal-times together can also give us a new understanding of evangelism. Proclaiming the good news of Jesus Christ is frequently seen as going out with a brief, well-rehearsed pitch that is supposed to reach peo-ple. But our sharing of God's good news can also be a natural outgrowth of our experience of his gifts. Evangelism is not just giving a preplanned speech made up by someone else, but is also a burst of joy coming from the depths of our beings as we share at the Lord's table. Our proclamation of Jesus as Lord can be like the spontaneous appreciation voiced at a delicious home-cooked meal. When we experience God's presence in the whole of our lives, we become eager to invite others to his table. Not even the most hardened of cynics would object to such a God or reject such an invitation.

When we look at nutrition from the perspective of enjoyment and celebration, some wonderful things can happen. For example, as we learn to eat quality foods that are fresh and without additives, the ex-perience of eating can generate a rebirth experience. We can discover just how good a home-grown to-mato can taste, or have the incomparable enjoyment of a good drink of spring water after strenuous exer-cise, or the contentment accompanying a well-prepared, home-cooked meal. Each takes on a deeply spiritual quality. Saying grace may no longer be just a rote exercise, but a natural response to the goodness of creation, tasted and relished. Instead of being marked by hurry, guilt, and indigestion, our eating can be full of thanks, love, and praise.

Experiences and exercises

1. Keep a list of what you eat this week. See if there is a pattern to it. How much do you eat? When do you eat? Why do you eat?

2. Instead of (or in addition to) a prayer before your meals, offer a prayer *after* eating, expressing how your meal makes you feel.

3. Look at the following list of common physical problems: headaches, stomach disorders, constipation, tiredness, lack of energy, edginess, irritability, sleeplessness. If you suffer from any of these, might improved nutrition increase your state of health?

4

The Body and Movement

No matter what our age or physical condition, most of us have moments when we imagine ourselves to be physically fit and perfectly coordinated. We begin to daydream. We fantasize our bodies moving across a football field, gliding on a dance floor, or swinging from a trapeze. You may have such a recurring fantasy. You may have even acted on it and amazed yourself at the abilities you actually do have. If you haven't acted on your dream, or if there's another dream you would like to work on, perhaps the following pages will be of help. There are many books available on how to exercise. But for most of us, the bigger difficulty is finding the motivation to exercise. We need help in taking those first halting, clumsy, and painful steps. With this in mind we offer the following suggestions on getting moving and staying moving. When you do, we guarantee that you will never be the same person again.

Why exercise

Together with psychiatrists Thaddeus Kostrubala and William Glasser and a growing list of experts, we firmly believe that "to be alive is to move." Why exercise? The answer is simple—for your life! Movement is basic to our very humanity. It is coded into our genes, molded into our coronary arteries and neural pathways, and shaped into our bones, muscles, and joints. Life began when the Spirit *moved* creatively over the waters (Genesis 1). Human life begins when God breathes the breath of life into us (Genesis 2). To be alive, to be animated, is to be filled with breath.

Today we no longer move very much under our own power. Instead, we are moved about. As a result we lose something. We become less alive and less animated. Movement makes us grow and brings us closer to the source of life, the moving Spirit of God. God's active Spirit is as close as a walk in the woods, a run on the beach, a ride on a horse, or a swim in the ocean—as close as our bodies themselves. As Paul exclaimed, "Yet he is not far from each one of us, for 'In him we live and *move*, and have our being'" (Acts 17:27-28, italics added).

We need to define briefly what we mean by exercise. *Significant physical exercise* involves more than just movement. For example, while walking has value, walking for exercise needs to be vigorous if it is to attain the highest benefits. These benefits are achieved only when a certain level of heart and lung activity is reached and maintained. Significant exercise involves varying amounts of the following components: *mode* (running, biking, walking, swimming), *intensity* (60% to 90% of maximal heart rate), *frequency* (3-5 times a week), *duration* (15-60 continuous minutes), and *initial level of fitness* (the higher the fitness, the more the exercise). Each part and its amount depends on your level of fitness. Significant physical exercise involves your heart and lungs. That generally means at least 15 minutes of exercise, three times a week.

Many homemakers, when asked about the exercise they get, would reply: "I get plenty of exercise, going up and down the stairs as I cook, clean, and keep house." Working at home is by no means easy. But the kind of exertion a contemporary homemaker makes in a typical day may not be the best exercise. It may in fact be harmful. If a person is a little overweight, has any history of heart problems, and does such exercise in particularly hot weather or for unusually long periods of time, such so-called exercise can result in a heart attack. At the least, a lowering of resistance may make it easier for other health problems to occur. The same is true for the kind of exercise many business people engage in after work. Many slightly paunchy office workers proudly announce that they are playing handball once or twice a week. They may rightly be proud of their determination, but they may not be so prudent in their choice of exercise. For an out-of-shape business person to rush onto a handball court or into any form of hard physical exercise without a gradual conditioning program is an invitation to trouble.

Before embarking on any fitness program, it is wise to consult with a physician. It is also helpful to talk with a health professional who has a good understanding of exercise. One wonders about the credibility of an overweight, hypertensive, choleric doctor. If you can find a doctor who is acquainted with sports medicine, you are likely to get good counsel concerning exercise. Such physicians know what high-level wellness is as opposed to average wellness. Second, *begin gradually.* Overdoing it at the start almost always guarantees a quick stop. Third, *pick a physical activity appropriate to your body type.* This is not to say you can't change or cross boundaries. Just be aware of the kind of exercise you are doing. In all that you do, let your body be your guide. In choosing your activity, look at your body. In the amount of exercise that you do, listen to your body's signals about overstress. As you increase your level of activity, monitor your body

messages and begin to learn what this great teacher
suggests as the best way for you.

Why not exercise?

Before dealing with the positive aspects of exercise, we have to be realistic about the multitude of
resistances to such experiences. There are a variety
of reasons why we choose not to exercise. Some are
good ones, others are not. What follows is a list of
three typical resistances to exercise. This first set
consists of excuses we use which are basically personal in nature. You may hear some familiar ones.

• *"I'm out of shape."* The most common and rather honest response is, "I'm out of shape." Usually we
begin by saying we are overweight. Then we proceed
to bemoan the fact that we have no breath. "I can't
run two blocks without being out of breath." The
list of "out-of-shape" or "pardon-me-but-I-can't" re-
sponses is endless. We have become expert at excus-
ing ourselves. How do we respond to this problem?
First of all, let's admit that we are *all* out of shape.
Ask Boston Marathon winner Bill Rogers if he is
really in shape and he would give you a list of ail-
ments, aches, and pains a mile long. Fitness is rela-
tive. None of us is in the shape we could be in or
want to be in. Each of us is less fit than some and
more fit than others. For that reason it is important
not to begin comparing ourselves with superstars.

Such an initial comparison invites early disappointment. Begin where you are.

A rule of thumb for general exercise is, "Train but don't strain." For example, many people get breathless the minute they start jogging. Dr. George Sheehan suggests they run slowly enough so that they can talk to someone as they go. Not only will the pace be reasonable, but the companionship and conversation will be an extra bonus. Remember, we all have a long way to go!

● *"Do I have to exercise?"* Some people exercise for the wrong reasons. They do it because they feel they have to. Whether imposed from the outside by some authority figure (a doctor, society, or peer pressure) or from the inside by a compulsive ego, the result is often the same. After a noble start and a short burst of exercise, they quit. Their jogging, swimming, or tennis-playing becomes only a good memory and a resolution for next year. Why is this so often the case? The apostle Paul wrote, "when the commandment came, sin revived and I died" (Rom. 7:9). We human beings will only follow rules for a short time. If these do not somehow become internalized or personalized, we quickly abandon them. Unless we decide that we *want* to continue and even *enjoy* what we are doing, the effort will be painful and short-lived.

It is prudent, therefore, to choose a form of exercise that you enjoy. Also, set realistic and realizable goals. At the beginning, don't attempt to exercise every day. Pick times in advance when nothing will come along and interfere or interrupt. Select partners to share in the experience. In addition to their companionship, you will give each other the little extra push needed when you just don't feel like exercising. With a little consistency and regularity, you will in time find motivation that is internal and lasting.

• *"I don't have time."* The third excuse is the simple conversation stopper, "I don't have time for that." As supporting evidence we usually cite such things as work obligations and family commitments. When someone says they don't have the time, what they are really saying is that *they don't want to make the time.* Most likely such persons simply don't want to exercise. If so, they should be honest with themselves. Each of us has as much or as little time as we decide to give to the various activities of our lives. If something is important enough to us, we will find the time to do it.

One hour a day isn't too much time to give to our bodies. Actually that is a very small amount of time in view of the hours we give to our minds, jobs, families, and others. Our bodies deserve at least one hour a day of good, vigorous exercise. If we are just starting out, we may not even want to take a full hour. The human body is a once-in-a-lifetime gift. It is the best and most priceless home we will ever possess. It is the finest and most efficient means of transportation available. It is the temple of the Holy Spirit.

The next set of resistances are "sports problems." They are characteristics of sports in our society, and their strong influence makes it increasingly difficult for us to get going and stay going with exercise.

• *Superstars and pros.* The definition of sports in our society has grown so narrow that most people are excluded. Once upon a time, most sports or games were participated in by anyone who wanted to get involved. But with the advent of professional teams, high salaries, media hype, and superstars, there is now little room for average athletes except in front of their TV sets, sitting in comfortable chairs and drinking beer.

Fortunately, some exciting new grass-roots developments hold promise for a renaissance of participatory games. The best-known is the concept of New Games, initiated by Stewart Brand. These guarantee that everyone joins, everyone has fun, and no one gets hurt. Wonderfully playful games have been created using such outlandish equipment as gigantic earth balls, parachutes, throwaway softballs, and knee socks. Infinity Volleyball is especially fun. Using a huge earth ball, the object of the game is not to beat the other side, but to see how many times a team can hit the ball back and forth. The game re-

quires teamwork and cooperation, because it is impossible for one person—even the strongest—to move the ball alone. The laughter is uproarious. The competition is intense. The sense of drama and the thrill of being involved produce a warm glow at the end of each tournament.

• *"Winning is everything."* Sports have in many ways been whittled down to a simple formula: win or lose. It doesn't really make any difference how you play, it's the results that count. Vince Lombardi—who has been virtually canonized as the saint of professional football—summed it all up when he bellowed, "Winning isn't everything. It's the *only* thing!" Such mottos can inspire some exceptional performances, but this win-lose syndrome can be hideous in its effects. Not only are adults discouraged from beginning sports and exercise, but young children often burn out in Little League Baseball and Pop-Warner Football even before their adolescence has ended. George Leonard and others have proposed a return to sports and exercise as recreation, as experiences which are rewards in themselves.

• *"Dumb jock."* Physical education is often characterized as unintellectual. Laboring under this stereotype and stigma, P.E. is typically viewed as an elective. Do you remember all the elaborate excuses schoolgirls would devise to get out of P.E.? This may have been because of some negative experiences, but it is also a sad commentary on our society's

enslaving view that women are not to be physical.
Most of us have painful recollections of gym class.
Remember that horrible process by which teams
were selected? If you were not the first or second
chosen, then you were an extra, a nobody. Again,
George Leonard has a hopeful alternative vision. Re-
minding us of the historic role of the gymnasium
in the liberal arts, he proposes that we once again
elevate P.E. to its rightful place in the educational
process. Physical education can integrate every field
of learning, for all observation, learning, and growth
begins with the body.

• *"You mean it's supposed to be fun?"* In sports
and exercise we have all too often been oriented
toward extrinsic rather than intrinsic rewards. Rather
than enjoying an activity for its own sake, we enjoy
it because of some prize at the end. Further, we look
on the quantity of things we do—the number of miles
we run, the number of sit-ups we do, or the number
of minutes we meditate—rather than simply enjoying those moments of movement. Movement can be
enjoyed simply in and of itself. It is a precious gift
of God to enrich our lives here and now.

Nine visions of exercise

Much of what we are doing in this book is a
process of deepening and broadening definitions.
We are pointing out the spiritual dimensions of

various body experiences. We would now like to offer nine old and new visions for expanding our understanding of exercise.

• *Exercise as health.* Physical health affects more than just the body. It affects the mind and spirit as well. Most of us have a relatively low level of physical health, and we experience the consequences of that in how well we think and feel. If we are concerned about the health of our whole selves, we need to take care of our bodies, and that means exercise.

• *Exercise as fitness.* Through regular exercise, things can happen to our bodies that are almost miraculous. Most people are aware of the weight control that often accompanies consistent physical conditioning. But few people know that through one year of regular, daily jogging they can almost double their capillary capacity. Think of it! In one year, your body could be serviced by twice as many circuits. In many instances, after several years of regular running, your pulse rate at rest could be one-half that of an average person. Your heart would then be working only about half as hard. Many other physical evidences of fitness can be cited: clearer skin, shinier hair, rosier cheeks, firmness of muscles, regularity, and an improved sex life. The list goes on and on. You could see and experience such exciting body changes! And as your heart and lungs are strengthened on a physical level, you will begin to see how your spiritual capacities for life and action increase as well.

• *Exercise as flexibility.* Exercise is more than just strength, speed, and endurance. One frequently overlooked aspect is flexibility. Flexibility has long been recognized as necessary for safe exercise. But it is now being seen as important in its own right. One type of yoga teaches that flexibility is not just physical limberness, but also spiritual relaxation. Think for a moment of people you know whose bodies seem tense. Aren't they often the same people who are uptight in other ways? Various forms of exercise which increase physical flexibility can also expand our spiritual awareness and can have a soothing effect that lasts long afterward.

• *Exercise as a natural high.* Exercise is a "high," a natural, nonpharmaceutical high. Have you ever experienced a "second wind"? You had been engaging in hard exercise and were just about ready to quit, when suddenly you got a rush of energy. The stimulant responsible for this sensation is epinephrine ("adrenalin"), a hormone which is a superenergizer. In his studies of distance runners, Kostrubala discovered that this hormone is usually released after 20-30 minutes of vigorous physical activity, bringing a burst of strength and a good feeling. What a wonderful safety valve and pleasure creator to have built into our bodies! There is no hangover, no dependency, and no physical degeneration. But unlike un-

natural highs, this one cannot be bought, controlled, or manipulated. It is not automatic. Instead it comes only after physical sacrifice and only when it is needed. It happens when you have paid your physical dues. It's a bit like the line from the spiritual that says, "If you don't bear the cross, then you can't wear the crown." But believe us, it is well worth it!

• *Exercise as pleasure.* One of the benefits of exercise is simply the pleasure that can come from regular physical activity. For example, after a certain amount of movement, all one's senses are heightened. One becomes acutely aware, seeing ordinary things as if for the first time. One may smell new fragrances in the air. Hyacinth bushes along the road may glow as if the branches were capped with fire. The combination of smell, sight, and sound is electrifying! Exercise has a way of cleaning out all the clogged sensory pores of our bodies so that we can experience the wonderful riches of life around us. It can help us understand something of what the church father Irenaeus meant when he said, "The glory of God is people fully alive."

• *Exercise as adventure.* In the western world our vision has generally been directed outward. This has often caused us to overlook the inward journey into our bodies. Exercise can provide a unique opportunity to go on "body adventures" and explore mental landscapes. Each time one exercises there is always new territory to explore and probe as well as old familiar haunts to revisit.

● *Exercise as self-knowledge.* Our bodies are excellent teachers; they do not lie. They can also be our best friends and companions. But they need to be well-treated, and that means they must be exercised. The more fit we become, the clearer our body speaks to us and the more it tells us of life, of people, and of God. It tells us with crystal clearness all that is going on around us—in sights, smells, tastes, and sensations. The more we exercise, the stronger and more understandable are the signals our feelings and emotions give. We become more aware of both outer and inner realities. It is vital to keep our bodies in good repair. Like sleek, well-built machines, they are meant to move. And when they do, they give good and reliable information about us.

● *Exercise as therapy.* The use of running as an adjunct to other forms of therapy has had significant results in terms of addiction problems, schizophrenia, and depression. But of much greater applicability to most people is the simple self-therapy which occurs through movement and exercise. Running can relieve tension, help us work through anger, and build emotional endurance and confidence. Through rhythmic, flowing movement, locked parts of us become unstuck, and knotty problems are loosened. It is not uncommon to begin a run with a particularly complicated problem weighing us down and find that, during the run, answers or possible solutions literally pop into our minds. Similar experiences of healing sometimes happen through swimming, dancing, and even weight lifting.

• *Exercise as community.* One of the most important and enjoyable aspects of regular exercise is companionship. This experience is well-known to anyone who has been a part of a team or struggled with another person through a difficult time. Sometimes in running, biking, walking, swimming, or dancing with a partner, common ground is discovered out of shared pain, exhaustion, and peak experiences. Barriers begin to break down. Much of the restrictive tightness that keeps us from growing closer together disappears. Through exercise together we can become the kindred spirits that God intends us to be.

Experiences and exercises

1. Monitor your body weight closely during the week and compare your weight change with changes in your self-image.

2. If you do not now exercise regularly, list the reasons why not. Examine them closely. Are the reasons you have listed the real ones, or are there others? Be honest with yourself.

3. Think of some times in your life when you found joy and pleasure in hard physical exercise.

What was it about those times that you found enjoyable?

4. Explore a new form of exercise this week and record your feelings about it.

5. Think of one person who might be willing to exercise with you on a regular basis. Invite them to do so.

5

The Body
and Play

As children, our days were filled with dreams of one adventure after another. Together with other playmates, we would scramble through our imaginary worlds. We built forts, played house, climbed trees, dressed up, and made rope swings. We explored vacant lots, made secret journeys into forbidden neighborhoods, broke windows, and generally put a scare into our parents. When we weren't playing games of fantasy, we were playing hide-and-seek, tag, follow-the-leader, or catch. The list of games was endless, just like our dreams and energies. We ran, we fell, and we ran some more.

Those days were far from perfect. There was competition, defeat, and hurt feelings. Yet they were still times for everyone to dream and to use their bodies in playing out those fantasies. They provided us storehouses of cherished memories. Those dreams of glory and adventure helped us grow. Through them we began to act out our developing values and personalities.

As adults we still dream. But we rarely act out our dreams and resolve them through physical activity. Instead, they either stay in our minds or are projected onto others. There is something harmful in that. A satisfying resolution of a dream often comes only when we are able to bodily enter into it and work it out.

Our ancestors knew their own needs very well when they developed detailed rites and rituals for various situations and times. They were thus able to act out their deepest hopes and fears, and in a very satisfying way entered into the reality behind the ritual. Their fears were resolved, their anxieties were dissipated, and they discovered new strength to carry on. It was not necessary to actually live out these things. It was enough to participate in their reality through play-acting.

Most of us like to pretend that we are too sophisticated for that sort of thing. Dressing up in unusual costumes and involving ourselves in ancient rituals seems a bit farfetched. But are we really so distant from such play? Think back to the last wedding you attended. Most likely there were some rather peculiar costumes and some ancient rituals going on, not to mention some pretty powerful hopes and fears wrapped up in all the festivity. Our lives today are filled with such rituals, no less than the lives that our ancestors lived.

One of the sad things about modern Americans, however, is that we are physically acting out our dreams less and less. We are increasingly becoming spectators to our own lives, as we sit in front of our TV sets, projecting our emotions onto our favorite teams or characters in a soap opera. This kind of involvement is far less satisfying than physical activity, and certainly contributes little to our overall state of health. We need to find ways to increase our physical involvement in the acting out of our deepest dreams.

The church's liturgy has preserved a highly meaningful drama of salvation in which we can participate. Too often we enter worship services with our hearts and minds on other things, never fully appreciating what is going on. Too often we remain spectators. One way to make worship more meaningful for us is to become more aware of the dramatic, even playful, aspect of the liturgy.

We are not here advocating that sort of playing at worship that Gordon Dahl criticizes in his book, *Work, Play, and Worship in a Leisure-Oriented Society*. He rightly admonishes us not to be superficial about worship. If we are flippant, irrelevant, preoccupied, disjointed, and hesitant about it, then we are just going through meaningless motions and emotions. Worship must be clear, sensitive, coherent, relevant, and involve all of us. Only in this way can its playful aspect be properly appreciated.

Christ is alive and in our midst in the church's liturgy. In our Sunday morning gatherings we enact a reality that is for every day, for all time. It is full of awe and mystery, wonder and rejoicing. The processions, readings, music, preaching, and sacraments are powerful communicators of God's word to us. The announcement of God's deliverance sends our hearts leaping. We are set free to live and play in God's grace! As the drama ends, we are sent into the world to serve others, not because we have to, but because we want to.

To help you become more aware of the playful aspect of worship, try the following exercise the next time you attend a worship service: Imagine yourself participating in the liturgy as a dancer or a mime. As each part of the drama unfolds, try to capture the feelings in imaginary physical movements. When you hear the words of forgiveness, what would your body naturally do? First identify the feeling, then picture how your body would respond. Imagine how you would express your joy at being invited to the Lord's Table. When the service is over, reflect back on your imaginings. Did they increase your attentiveness and help you participate more fully in the service? Are there ways that your congregation

might become outwardly more involved in the liturgy as well as inwardly? You may wish to discuss your thoughts with your pastor or congregational worship committee.

Since ancient times, the Christian liturgy has acted out the deepest hopes of the church. And in a very real way, that dramatic action has given Christians increased knowledge and experience of their Lord and a taste of God's coming kingdom.

Toward a broader sense of play

Church services are not the only places where we can increase our physical involvement through play. God has created a whole world for us to appreciate and explore. Our childhood experiences of play should be seen as just the beginning of a lifetime of adventure in our world. Our play can take an infinite variety of forms.

For many people, the term *play* sounds too childish. They prefer terms like *recreation* and *leisure.* These are more meaningful in some ways, but they are also very narrowly defined today. Recreation is usually seen as what we do when our work is done, our studies are completed, and our house is cleaned. Weekends or evenings are the times for it. The mountains, the park, or the beach are the places. Recreation requires all sorts of equipment—sometimes elaborate and frightfully expensive. If not bats, balls, and gloves, it's sailboats, motorcycles, and RV's.

There are real problems with such an approach. For one thing, what if it's impossible to get away? Given the energy shortage and restricted budgets, it is very difficult for many people to get to their favorite retreats. And what if one cannot get outdoors or has no access to the customary equipment? Finally, we don't always have two to three hours or a whole afternoon at our disposal. Suppose there is only a portion of an hour available? In most cases we would either let the time slip by, or else settle for the TV and a cold beer. We lose any benefits we might have received through re-creating ourselves in that time.

If we are going to use the term *recreation,* we have to understand it in its broad sense. We can re-create ourselves anywhere, anytime, and with no equipment. Any number of activities will do. The important thing is that we make use of the opportunities that we have, and not wait for our lives to be in perfect order before we begin. In order for recreation to be truly helpful, it needs to be more than just a once-a-year scramble during our vacation time. It needs to be part of our everyday life-style and discipline.

The concept of *leisure* has similar problems. It is a uniquely American phenomenon of the 20th century. The customary two-day weekend is growing into a three-day weekend. And with it is growing the need to know what to do with all the extra time. For many, that time is important because their work is an increasingly pressure-laden drudgery. But because we have few productive expectations of our leisure time, we tend to see it as "wasted time," in contrast to our working time, which is supposedly more intrinsically valuable.

To one degree or another, all of us have become victims of compartmentalized living. One compartment is for sleeping, another for eating, another for family, and still another for work. Recreation and leisure are supposed to fit in somewhere, though we're not really sure where.

We need a new vision of what leisure and recreation are all about. They are not additions to an already busy life, but are rather the ways we go about our lives themselves, whatever we are engaged in. Leisure may happen during one's morning bathroom routine, while driving to work, in the midst of housework, or at any other moment. Five minutes of such leisure may be more beneficial than a whole day of so-called leisure activity.

Because all time and all life is a gift from God, we needn't constantly rush and hurry to prove ourselves, to accomplish something, to produce or reach a goal. Leisure is a response to the knowledge that we have been forgiven, accepted, and blessed. This realization brings with it rest, patience, and acceptance.

It transforms whatever quantity of time that is available to us into quality time.

So many of us allow ourselves to be pressured by the seeming shortness of time. We have too many things to do, and too little time in which to do them. So we grow anxious. The pressure builds. We rush through the day, getting this or that done. But we see that we cannot finish it all in the time that is given us. So we add tomorrow's anxiety to today's unfinished business. And we dream, yearning for that ideal moment of leisure when we may rest, recuperate, and let the rest of ourselves catch up with the frantic pace we've run.

Leisure is our deliverance from that trap. We halt that chaotic, spinning confusion of inner anxieties. We center ourselves on the moment that we are living right now. We think not about what we failed to do yesterday or what we must get done tomorrow, but about now. The consequences of such an attitude can be a nearly miraculous lengthening of the quality of our days, similar to the feeling many of us had during summers of our youth. Days were full, and time was gloriously unending. We lived in the present. The same is possible for us today.

Learning to play again

Many people have forgotten how to play, to re-create, or to be leisurely. Life's burdens and responsibilities have covered their natural talent under years of scars. As a way of tying together the major themes of this book, we offer the following suggestions for recovering a healthy sense of play. We hope they will aid you in seeing life from the perspective of joy in God's creation, and in entering into a fulfilling relationship with that creation through your body spirituality.

• *Consider sport as art.* Sport was not originally designed for one person to improve his or her self-esteem by destroying someone else's. As the early Greeks understood it, sport was an art form. The underlying goals were to develop the body to its fullest potential, to improve the mind through better health, and to enrich the spirit through exercise. Greek sculpture bears ample testimony to the beauty, grace, and magnificence of the human body engaged in sport. Sport has an esthetic dimension which need not become idolatry, as so often happens today. Modern sports heroes are honored as conquerors rather than as artists. It's time we looked at all sports as playful activities with their own beauty, grace, and integrity.

• *Stimulate your senses.* Tune in to your external senses of touch, taste, smell, sight, and hearing. Become more receptive to the beauty and wonder of your environment. Develop your internal senses as well. Our nervous systems are marvelously complex communications networks. You'll be awed by the millions of messages that we ordinarily overlook. Note, too, how prematurely we judge so many sensations to be negative. Hunger pangs, for example, are much too often interpreted negatively. So we rush to our refrigerators to eliminate them. If we would calmly stay with the feeling for awhile, it might turn out to be a neutral, normal body sensation which soon goes away on its own.

• *Practice concentration.* Focus your thoughts. Clear your mind, as best you can, of the constant turmoils of daily living. Having many thoughts on your mind at one time dissipates valuable energies. By concentrating on one thought only, you in effect pull yourself together.

• *Play regularly.* Haphazard and infrequent efforts at play have similar results. Pleasant experiences are rare. Pain and discomfort are more frequent. Further, the lack of regularity makes it easier to put off until tomorrow what you had planned to do today. If your activity becomes boring, try another! Be creative. Vary your environment or time of day. Morning activities have a very different feel to them than those of the early evening.

• *Be cooperative, not competitive.* Life is already altogether far too competitive for us to make our play into contests as well. Competition leads to only one winner. The rest are losers. Instead of viewing other participants as competitors, think of them as partners in the game. Instead of trying to humiliate your opponents, seek to stretch their abilities. Challenge them, don't compete with them.

• *Enjoy the moment.* Stay in the here and now. Beware of the carrot-in-front-of-the-donkey syndrome. Get something out of this activity at this moment in time. Avoid the mindset that says, "I'll be better for it someday." You will be better for it today, and you need not worry about tomorrow. If you find yourself thinking about what you're going to do right after you take a shower, you know right away that you are not in the here and now.

• *Evaluate, don't criticize.* It is common for us to yell at ourselves, "Oh, what a stupid play, you idiot!" For many of us, self-depreciation comes naturally. We need to remember that the value of what we are doing is not derived from how much better we are than someone else. Instead of criticizing yourself, evaluate yourself by asking the following questions:

Is this personally fun?

Do I enjoy my partner, who may also be my opponent?

How does the environment add or detract from this experience? What could I do to enrich it?

Do I enjoy the motion of the activity? Is my body movement smooth or graceful? Does it have an even, rhythmic flow? Or is it rough and halting?

Does this refresh me or oppress me? Why?

How might I economize or shorten the motion of

my body to make it more meaningful? How might I broaden or expand it?

• *Listen to your inner voice.* Monitor the messages of your various body parts. Put them together and observe how they construct a total body picture. Notice what seems to be working in harmony. What is frustrating your sense of wholeness?

• *Relax and rest.* Know when to stop and smell the flowers. Pause frequently. Walk slowly, or sit down and briefly meditate. Pray. Give yourself the gift of time daily. Build playfulness into your day.

• *Expect to be refreshed.* The more definite your expectations, the more satisfied you will be. Being alert for the here-and-now reward will make you more aware of the refreshment that is there.

• *Use your imagination.* Dream. Explore. Experiment. Take nothing for granted. Even the commonplace may be ripe with recreational opportunities.

• *Learn from children.* Children are the experts. They are the masters of play from whom we can learn. Watch them become completely absorbed in pots and pans from under the kitchen sink. Notice how they prefer an empty cardboard box to newly manufactured playhouses. They can play anytime, anywhere, and in any way. Learn, too, from the recollections of your own childhood. Uncover that treasure chest of youthful creativity, and learn to draw from it the riches that are inside.

Experiences and exercises

1. Do something with the only purpose in mind being enjoyment. What is something that you have wanted to do, but haven't? Do it!

2. Do some physical activity that requires no equipment.

3. Consciously pick a moment to play at work. Build some playfulness into a different activity each day.

4. Each day this week, use five minutes doing *nothing*. What do you experience in your body during that time? How do you feel afterward?

5. List activities that are recreative for you.

Bibliography

Allen, Dorothy J., and Fahey, Brian W., eds. *Being Human in Sport*. Philadelphia: Lea & Febiger, 1977.

Benjamin, Alice, and Corrigan, Harriett. *Cooking with Conscience*. New York: Seabury Press, 1977.

Berkeley Holistic Health Center. *The Holistic Health Handbook*. Berkeley: And/Or Press, 1978.

Berrigan, Daniel. *Love, Love at the End*. New York: The Macmillan Company, 1971.

Braaten, Carl E., and Braaten, LaVonne. *The Living Temple*. New York: Harper & Row, 1976.

Brokering, Herbert. *I Opener*. St. Louis: Concordia, 1974.

Cargas, Harry James, and Lee, Bernard, eds. *Religious Experience and Process Theology*. New York: Paulist Press, 1976.

Conze, Edward. *Buddhist Meditation*. New York: Harper & Row, 1969.

Cox, Harvey. *The Seduction of the Spirit*. New York: Simon & Schuster, 1974.

Dahl, Gordon. *Work, Play, and Worship in a Leisure-Oriented Society*. Minneapolis: Augsburg, 1972.

Einstein, Albert. *Cosmic Religion* (out of print).

Fenton, John Y., ed. *Theology and Body*. Philadelphia: Westminster Press, 1974 (out of print).

Flengelman, Andrew, ed. *The New Games Book*. New York: Doubleday, 1976.

Flew, Antony, ed. *Body, Mind and Death*. New York: The Macmillan Company, 1964.

Fox, Matthew. *On Becoming a Musical, Mystical Bear*. New York: Paulist Press, 1972.

Fox, Matthew. *Whee! We, Wee All the Way Home*. Wilmington, N.C.: McGrath Publishing Co., 1977.

Gallen, John, ed. *Christians at Prayer*. Notre Dame, Ind.: University of Notre Dame Press, 1977.

Gallwey, W. Timothy. *The Inner Game of Tennis*. New York: Random House, 1974.

Glasser, William. *Positive Addiction*. New York: Harper & Row, 1976.

Hanh, Thich Nhat. *The Miracle of Being Awake*. Nyack, N.Y.: Fellowship Books, 1975.

Hanson, Richard S. *The Future of the Great Planet Earth*. Minneapolis: Augsburg, 1972.

Henderson, Joe, ed. *The Runner's Diet*. Mountain View, Calif.: Runner's World, 1972.

Henderson, Joe, ed. *Food for Fitness*. Mountain View, Calif.: World Publications, 1975.

Higdon, Hal, ed. *The Complete Diet Guide*. Mountain View, Calif.: World Publications, 1978.

Illich, Ivan D. *Celebration of Awareness*. New York: Doubleday, 1971.

Jourard, Sidney M. *The Transparent Self*. 2nd ed. New York: Van Nostrand Reinhold Co., 1971.

Keen, Sam. *To a Dancing God.* New York: Harper & Row, 1970.

Kopp, Sheldon B. *If You Meet the Buddha on the Road, Kill Him!* New York: Bantam, 1976.

Kostrubala, Thaddeus. *The Joy of Running.* New York: J. B. Lippincott, Co., 1976.

Lappe, Frances Moore. *Diet for a Small Planet.* Rev. ed. New York: Ballantine, 1975.

Lappe, Frances Moore, and Collins, Joseph. *Food First.* New York: Ballantine, 1979.

Leonard, George. *The Ultimate Athlete.* New York: Viking Press, 1975.

Leonard, George. *Education and Ecstasy.* New York: Dell Publishing Co., 1969.

Leonard, George. "Winning Isn't Everything." *Faith at Work,* LXXXVII, no. 4, June 1974.

Longacre, Dorothy. *More-with-Less Cookbook.* Scottsdale, Pa.: Herald Press, 1976.

Miller, Don Ethan. *Bodymind: The Whole Person Health Book.* Englewood Cliffs, N.J.: Prentice-Hall, Inc., 1975.

Missildine, W. Hugh. *Your Inner Child of the Past.* New York: Simon & Schuster, 1963.

Murphy, Michael. *Golf in the Kingdom.* New York: Dell Publishing Co., 1973.

Murphy, Michael. *Jacob Attabet: A Speculative Fiction.* New York: Bantam, 1979.

Nelson, James B. *Embodiment: An Approach to Sexuality and Christian Theology.* Minneapolis: Augsburg, 1978.

Nouwen, Henri J. M. *Creative Ministry.* New York: Doubleday, 1971.

Pelletier, Kenneth R. *Mind as Healer Mind as Slayer.* New York: Dell Publishing Co., 1977.

Pittenger, Norman. *Praying Today.* Grand Rapids, Mich.: William B. Eerdmans Publishing Co., 1974 (out of print).

Pollock, Michael L. "How Much Exercise Is Enough?" *The Physician and Sports Medicine,* June 1978.

Robinson, John A. T. *The Body: A Study in Pauline Theology.* Philadelphia: Westminster Press, 1977.

Sapp, Stephen. *Sexuality, the Bible and Science.* Philadelphia: Fortress Press, 1977.

Sheehan, George A. *Dr. Sheehan on Running.* New York: Bantam, 1978.

Sheehan, George A. *Running and Being.* New York: Warner Books, 1978.

Siirala, Aarne. *Divine Humanness.* Philadelphia: Fortress Press, 1970 (out of print).

Spicker, Stuart F., ed. *The Philosophy of the Body: Rejections of Cartesian Dualism.* New York: Quadrangle/The New York Times Book Co., 1972.

Spino, Mike. *Beyond Jogging: The Innerspaces of Running.* Millbrae, Calif.: Celestial Arts, 1976.

Spino, Mike. *Running Home.* New York: Berkeley, 1977.

Strommen, Merton P., et al. *A Study of Generations.* Minneapolis: Augsburg, 1972.

Williams, Margery. *The Velveteen Rabbit.* New York: Doubleday, 1958.

Wolff, Hans Walter. *Anthropology of the Old Testament.* Philadelphia: Fortress Press, 1974.